BLAZERS

ALL ABOUT FANTASY CREATURES

Discover
HARPIES,
MINOTAURS,
AND
Other Mythical
Fantasy Beasts

by A.J. Sautter

CAPSTONE PRESS
a capstone imprint

Blazers Books are published by Capstone Press,
1710 Roe Crest Drive, North Mankato, Minnesota 56003
www.mycapstone.com

Library of Congress Cataloging-in-Publication data
Names: Sautter, Aaron, author.
Title: Discover harpies, minotaurs, and other mythical fantasy beasts / by A.J. Sautter.
Description: North Mankato, MN : Capstone Press, 2018. | Series: Blazers. All about
  fantasy creatures | Includes bibliographical references and index.
Summary: "In handbook format, describes the physical features, behavior,
  and habitat of mythical fantasy beasts"—Provided by publisher.
Identifiers: LCCN 2017002064 (print) | LCCN 2017014757 (ebook) |
  ISBN 9781515768531 (eBook PDF) | ISBN 9781515768364 (library binding)
  ISBN 9781515768401 (paperback)
Subjects: LCSH: Animals, Mythical—Juvenile literature.
Classification: LCC GR825 (ebook) | LCC GR825 .S2755 2018 (print) |
  DDC 398/.45—dc23
LC record available at https://lccn.loc.gov/2017002064

Editorial Credits
Bobbie Nuytten, designer; Wanda Winch, media researcher;
Laura Manthe, production specialist

Photo Credits
Capstone: Carlos Molinari, cover (bottom), 3, Collin Howard, 4, 19, 27, Jason Juta,
5, 9, 29, 32, Martin Bustamante, 13, 15, 21, 23, 28, Mike Nash, cover (top), 1 (top), 7,
Stefano Azzalin, 11, 25; Shutterstock: SergeyIT, cover (background), 1 (background),
Vuk Kostic, 17

Printed in the United States of America.
010364F17

TABLE OF CONTENTS

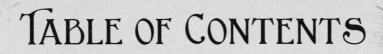

MYTHICAL FANTASY BEASTS!

Myths and legends are filled with friendly beasts such as unicorns or griffins. But in many stories, heroes faced harpies, minotaurs, and other deadly monsters. What would these mythical creatures be like if they were real? What would they eat? How would they behave? Let's find out!

myth—a story from ancient times; myths often tried to explain natural events

Fact: Ancient people believed sea serpents, griffins, and other mythical beasts were real living creatures.

CERBERUS

Size: 6.5 to 7 feet (2 to 2.1 meters) tall

Home: rocky plains and lava fields

Diet: none, it does not eat

Lifespan: unknown

Appearance: Cerberus appears as a huge, three-headed dog. Its feet are tipped with sharp claws. Its mouths are full of grinding teeth. And its eyes glow with burning fire.

Underworld—the place under the earth where ancient people believed the spirits of the dead went

lair—a hideout used by wicked people to keep their activities secret

Behavior: Cerberus is a cruel spirit that was given a physical form. A wicked wizard likely raised it from the **Underworld**. It spends most of its time guarding its master's secret **lair**. The beast can belch out balls of fire to burn intruders.

CHIMERAS

Size: 6.5 feet (2 m) tall, up to 15 feet (4.6 m) long
Home: dry caves in hilly areas
Diet: deer, sheep, wild pigs, rabbits, sometimes plants
Lifespan: unknown

Appearance: Most chimeras have the heads of a lion and a goat. A few also have a dragon's head. A large, poisonous snake forms a chimera's tail. Their front feet resemble dragon's claws. Their hind feet are goatlike hooves.

Behavior: Chimeras are beasts created by wicked gods or wizards. They are completely loyal to their creators. They obey orders without question. Chimeras with dragon heads sometimes enjoy attacking villages and collecting treasure.

GORGONS

Size: 5 to 5.5 feet (1.5 to 1.7 m) tall
Home: caves and ruined castles by the sea
Diet: rats, rabbits, frogs, fish, birds
Lifespan: unknown

Appearance: Most gorgons have scaly green skin. They have sharp fangs and a forked tongue. A gorgon's upper body looks like a human woman. Instead of hair, gorgons have a nest of squirming snakes on their heads.

Behavior: Gorgons were once beautiful women who were cursed by the gods. They live alone away from people. Gorgons use powerful magic to defend their homes. One look from a gorgon's glowing eyes can turn intruders into solid stone.

GRIFFINS

Size: 8.5 to 10 feet (2.6 to 3 m) long;
wingspans up to 25 feet (7.6 m)

Home: dry caves in grassy hills

Diet: rabbits, deer, sheep, camels, buffalo

Lifespan: 35 to 50 years

Appearance: Griffins have the large head,
wings, and **talons** of an eagle. Their lower
bodies have the powerful legs and sharp claws
of a lion. They are covered with a mix of
golden hair and feathers.

talon—a long, sharp claw

12

Behavior: Griffins usually live alone. They spend a lot of time flying and hunting for food. Griffins have incredible eyesight. They can spot prey up to 3 miles (5 kilometers) away. Some griffins are friendly and will help people who respect them.

Harpies

Size: 4 to 4.5 feet (1.2 to 1.4 m) tall; wingspans up to 9 feet (2.7 m)

Home: rocky cliffs and small caves near the sea

Diet: fish, crabs, seals, human sailors

Lifespan: about 40 years

Appearance: Harpies have the bodies of vultures. They have strong wings and feet tipped with sharp talons. Their heads appear as monstrous women. They have yellow eyes, greasy hair, and rotting teeth.

prey—an animal hunted by another animal for food

Behavior: Harpies never bathe. They reek from the bits of rotting flesh stuck to their filthy bodies. Harpies' favorite **prey** is human sailors. They use magical singing to cloud sailors' minds. The music draws sailors close to shore so harpies can attack.

Krakens

Size: more than 350 feet (107 m) long
Home: large caves on the ocean floor
Diet: fish, sharks, whales, human sailors
Lifespan: unknown

Appearance: Krakens look like gigantic squids or octopuses. They have tough, rubbery skin and ten **tentacles**. Krakens have wide mouths filled with swordlike teeth. Their large, 6-foot- (1.8-m-) wide eyes give them excellent vision.

> tentacle—a long, armlike body part some animals use to move, touch, or grab things

Behavior: Krakens enjoy fighting ships and the taste of human flesh. A kraken first crushes a ship in its huge tentacles. It then stuffs the doomed sailors into its mouth. It's thought that krakens age very slowly. They may live more than 1,000 years.

MINOTAURS

Size: 7.5 to 8 feet (2.3 to 2.4 m) tall

Home: mazelike networks of underground caves and tunnels

Diet: sheep, pigs, goats, goblins, humans

Lifespan: up to 300 years

Appearance: Minotaurs have legs and heads like a bull's. Their arms and **torsos** resemble a human's. They are covered in shaggy hair and have yellow eyes. They attack enemies and prey with sharp, deadly horns and claws.

torso—the part of the body between the neck and waist, not including the arms

Behavior: Minotaurs live alone in dark caves and tunnels. They have excellent vision and are fearsome hunters. They spend most of their time prowling for their next meal. Minotaurs have an amazing sense of direction. They never get lost in their dark, mazelike homes.

PEGASI

Size: 8.5 to 10 feet (2.6 to 3 m) long; wingspans up to 25 feet (7.6 m)

Home: forests and grassy plains

Diet: grass, oats, apples, carrots, beets

Lifespan: 50 to 70 years

Appearance: Pegasi have strong horselike bodies with powerful wings. They can fly up to 50 miles (80 km) per hour. They are usually white or light gray in color.

> **tame**—to train to live with and be useful to people

Behavior: Pegasi enjoy their freedom. They are not easily **tamed**. But they are good judges of character. They sometimes become friends with people who show them respect and kindness. Pegasi do not tolerate evil. They react violently toward wicked people.

PHOENIXES

Size: 10 to 12 feet (3 to 3.7 m) long; wingspans up to 30 feet (9 m)

Home: rocky cliffs in mountain regions

Diet: rabbits, sheep, goats, deer, warthogs

Lifespan: unknown

Appearance: Phoenixes are also called firebirds. They are covered in bright red feathers that glow with fire when they become angry. Phoenixes are strong enough to carry away an adult elephant.

Behavior: Phoenixes usually live far from humans. But they are noble creatures. They sometimes help wise wizards fight the forces of evil. When a phoenix reaches the end of its life, it bursts into flame. Then a newborn phoenix chick appears in the ashes.

Sea Serpents

Size: 150 to 200 feet (46 to 61 m) long
Home: warm oceans
Diet: fish, seals, squid, whales, human sailors
Lifespan: up to 500 years

Appearance: Also known as sea dragons, sea serpents have giant snakelike bodies covered in tough scales. They often have dragonlike heads and mouths filled with deadly teeth. Some also have large fins that look like dragon wings.

Behavior: Sea serpents spend most of their time hunting for prey. They will sometimes attack human ships. These giant creatures first coil their bodies around the ships to crush them. They then eat the doomed human sailors.

UNICORNS

Size: 8.5 to 10 feet (2.6 to 3 m) long

Home: grassy clearings in large forests

Diet: grass, ferns, berries, other leafy plants

Lifespan: more than 1,000 years

Appearance: Unicorns look similar to large white horses. These mythical creatures have bright blue or violet eyes. Their main feature is the magical **ivory** horn that grows from their heads. Evil wizards sometimes create powerful magic wands using unicorn horns.

> ivory—a hard, creamy-white material that makes up an animal's tusks or horns

Behavior: Unicorns are fierce protectors of the forest. They will quickly attack any wicked creature in the forest. Unicorns avoid humans. But they are friendly with elves, fairies, and other magical people.

Creature Quiz

1. You should never look into a gorgon's eyes because:

    A) you could lose your mind.
    B) you could be turned to stone.
    C) it's a sign of disrespect.

2. Unicorn horns are sometimes used to make:

    A) jewelry.
    B) small sculptures.
    C) powerful magic wands.

3. Which group of creatures may be friendly toward humans?

    A) griffins, pegasi, and phoenixes
    B) harpies, minotaurs, and unicorns
    C) Cerberus, griffins, and krakens

4. When a phoenix reaches the end of its life, it:

    A) flies across the ocean to its final resting place.
    B) bursts into flames and is reborn from the ashes.
    C) vanishes in a flash of light.

5. To trap their prey, harpies will often:

    A) use magic to appear as beautiful women.
    B) set up a large table full of food.
    C) sing magical songs to cloud sailors' minds.

6. A chimera has the body parts of which creatures?

   A) a horse, a lion, and an eagle

   B) a lion, a goat, a dragon, and a serpent

   C) a human, a vulture, and a bull

7. A Pegasus may help someone who:

   A) shows it kindness and respect.

   B) feeds it apples.

   C) is a magic user.

8. A minotaur never gets lost in its mazelike home because it:

   A) has excellent eyesight.

   B) has an excellent sense of direction.

   C) both A and B.

9. Cerberus looks like a huge, three-headed dog. But it is really:

   A) a cruel spirit from the Underworld.

   B) a monster created by a wicked wizard.

   C) a person under an evil curse.

10. Which of the following is a favorite food for both sea serpents and krakens?

   A) seals

   B) human sailors

   C) sharks

See page 31 for quiz answers.

Glossary

ivory (EYE-vur-ee)—a hard, creamy-white material that makes up an animal's tusks or horns

lair (LAYR)—a hideout used by wicked people to keep their activities secret

myth (MITH)—a story from ancient times; myths often tried to explain natural events

prey (PRAY)—an animal hunted by another animal for food

talon (TAL-uhn)—a long, sharp claw

tame (TAYM)—to train to live with and be useful to people

tentacle (TEN-tuh-kuhl)—a long, armlike body part some animals use to move, touch, or grab things

torso (TOR-soh)—the part of the body between the neck and waist, not including the arms

Underworld (UHN-dur-wurld)—the place under the earth where ancient people believed the spirits of the dead went

Read More

Hoena, Blake. *Theseus and the Minotaur: A Graphic Retelling*. Ancient Myths. North Mankato, Minn.: Capstone Press, 2015.

Osborne, Mary Pope, and Natalie Pope Boyce. *Dragons and Mythical Creatures*. Magic Tree House Fact Tracker. New York: Random House, 2015.

Sautter, A. J. *How to Draw Griffins, Unicorns, and Other Mythical Beasts*. Drawing Fantasy Creatures. North Mankato, Minn.: Capstone Press, 2016.

Quiz Answers:

1:B, 2:C, 3:A, 4:B, 5:C, 6:B, 7:A, 8:C, 9:A, 10:B

Internet Sites

Use FactHound to find Internet sites related to this book.

Visit *www.facthound.com*

Just type in 9781515768364 and go.

Check out projects, games and lots more at
www.capstonekids.com

Index